Mud Into Clay

Amanda Noel

BookLeaf Publishing

India | USA | UK

Presentation by *BookLeaf Publishing*

Web: www.bookleafpub.com

E-mail: info@bookleafpub.com

ISBN: 9789363311664

First edition 2024

For Eric, Becky, John, and myself: In loving memory of Mom and Dad.

For my hubby, Joe, my Mum and Dad-in-law, Paula and Joe, Ma and Carol:

In loving memory of Joseph V. Noel, Bruce, Bubba, and Bobby.

For Sharon: In loving memory of "Senior."

For Angela: In loving memory of David.

For Mike, Maria, and Analise: In loving memory of Anthony.

For April: In loving memory of "GG."

For Jamie and Deb: In loving memory of Barbara. ("Ma")

For Marielle, and all in the Brosnahan Clan: In loving memory of Kitty and Michelle

**Our loved ones are never truly lost from us, for their voices sing eternally in the Choir of the Roses.*

ACKNOWLEDGEMENT

Thanks to all who supported me the first time around: Joe, Paula and Joe, Carol, Becky (Thither) and Amro, John, Eric, Steph, Sharon and Jared, Sara (Opheilia), Kylie, Jamie, Deb, Missy, Pinky, April, Joel, Hunter, Adrielle, Becca (thanks especially for the desk, and the anthem "refuse to sink!"), Angela Marie, Mike and Maria ("Mama") Campinelli, Holly, Paul, and all in my extended family at Stephen King's Funking Friends, and- last, but never least- my four furry muses: Bali, Captain, Mo, and Eivor.

Special thanks go to the masters of lyrical inspiration: Mike Patton, Nivek Ogre, Edward KaSpel, Trent Reznor, M.J. Keenan, Ian Curtis, and Corpse Husband (to name just a "few" favorites). Without music, life would be unbearable.

...and thanks to all that I have forgotten to mention by name. You know who you are.

PREFACE

The majority of these poems were written between the years 2013 through 2017, and reflect just how difficult it can be to resurrect one's inner self after being numbed by the grief of losing a loved one(s). Uhm... enjoy? Or perhaps just save these verses for a rainy day when you need a good cry. Perception is everything.

Other books available by Amanda Noel:
Rivers of Autumn

Mourn

Only minutes till early morning
Yet the Sun still so far away
As the half-moon gleams with its insane smile
Accompanying these thoughts run astray
Windowpane frigid to numb fingertips
Somehow still warm against even colder lips
Frozen tears harden these icy eyes
For regrets unheard by uncaring skies

Seconds now till the morning
Burning with that name I cannot say
I should flee from these thoughts…
Get out while I can
For with the memories come the dismay
A zephyr of emotions trapped within my heart
Repressed pain that I dare not show
For a soul too dear to just simply depart
I mourn him more deeply than you'll ever know

Arriving at last, the early morning
Relentless minutes keep ticking away
In this bed lies the vexation of one who can't
sleep
To escape into dreams of happier days
Even knowing he's free, and in a better place

This grief far too great to be denied
His spectral palms still warm against my face
Heat that mirrors the fire I am holding inside

Fanatical

My void of defense… seems too perfect now
That Voice I hear, and speak to
Even when I know they're not really here
Spectral hands that support me; hold me high
Above all obstacles assailing me
Then a perception in my heart intervened…
We two could have become a wonderful thing
Is this what you might have seen
…or did you disagree?

A fanatical love was my one reality
And you "knew" that you could never set me
free
Nor did you try; understanding the why
This, I know, I see
Yet, you hover close to me
You've been here before; I still feel you
Somewhere in a distant memory
Your hand clutching at my shirtsleeve
Trembling against my shoulder
Is familiar, and more comforting
Than you ever wanted to know
Hopelessly, I fall for you… again
To consume this comfort as it grows

I sensed your shadow of uncertainty
The incessant question of how you made me feel
Secure and safe; a warm sheltered place
A feeling that always seemed to frighten me
Always… I could have loved you for that alone
Apprehensive woman; once a terrified little girl
That we both lost somehow along the way
You found her; brought her back once more
And I must thank you for that because I missed
her
She returned to life; resurrected by your light
That dawned the first time that you kissed her
I wonder… do you remember that very first time
When, so hesitant, you touched your lips to
mine?

Felt so much within, both burned by the taste
Despite of all that occurred, just this once
I will not regret acting upon impulsive haste
…could you have set me free?
I ask not of you, but of myself
I think now it could have been easy
More simple than I thought it could ever be
But you wouldn't have…
And never should have wanted to be
The one who could take those dreams away
from me

Reveling in the bond we both still hold so fond
...I felt that we should strive to keep it
So I hid my dysfunctional feeling away
With the hope that you'd never see it

evoL's Dire Need

So… this is how it all began
Or was it the beginning of my ending?
The end of a constant battle with sorrow
Or the start of still more despair pending
I plea for this anguish to not consume me
My words of emotion, finally spoken,
But my voice just passes you by like a breeze
Winds of heartache and promises broken

These "evoL" thoughts that you may have heard
But dared not process through your mind
Went about your tasks as though nothing were
wrong
Oblivious to what you had left behind
I fell out of step as you shouldered on
Knowing nothing of the agony I carried inside
 Unaware as I watched you from a distance
You'd see nothing of the potential you once
denied

Voices echo, amplified in that tiled cell
Sly, easy taunts, bounced back and forth with
bravado
How harmless it all seemed as I hid a crimson
flush

Disguising a secret smile beneath my visor's
shadow
And so natural it seemed for us to banter this
Such cruel sweetness of a dark temptation
Which we both believed would never come to
pass
And maybe it should have never… late
realization

But I could and would not deny
That blissful elation of the saccharine ache
That twisted itself around my heart
Every time you spoke my name
So, we took up the shovels into our hands
And kept digging ourselves further down
Deeper, and even deeper still
It seems we should have been in China by now

As the hole we toiled widened in the earth
So did my desperate yearning grow
Unable to even look you in the eye, for fear
Of that sea-blue gaze reflecting my desire's glow
Such sweet torment, I dreamed of taking you
As the loose tongues wagged, to say whatever
they will
Anytime, anywhere; consequences be damned
Just more breezes to turn the blades of the ol'
rumor mill

Yet with that desire, came the depiction of
shame
For who was I to crave your touch…
While someone waited for me at home?
…not that HE really cared for me all that much
And that torch I'd been holding for far too long
A shimmer beneath the mask that I wore
Fastidiously applied for too many years
Then you yielded to me, and I could hide no
more

And who knows what might have been for us?
Not you, and certainly not I
All we know is that what we both wanted
Has for whatever the reasons been denied
And I know that these words change nothing
now
They just make it harder to keep my anguish
inside
The cruel phrase spoken, "timing is everything"
So why was our timing always out of stride?

Oblivion

Wasted, faded… once optimistic view now jaded
Every thrill has long since gone
Yet somehow, still, she carries on

As her sweet oblivion remains
She has learned to embrace the pain
In her dreams each night, she ventures far
To take him for a stroll along the stars
Then, like punishment, arrives the dawn
Moonlight vanished, and he is gone
Apart again; he cannot hear her cries
As blinding sunlight pierces her eyes

Writhing, burning… every part of her is
yearning
Reaching for him, touching only his essence
So far away, but she can still feel his presence

Longing for overcasts, she prays for rain
To cleanse, and scour away the pain
Coping because there is no other choice
Enduring the emptiness without his voice
Still… the oblivion remains
And now she has come to loathe the pain
Only within dreams can they two be together
Such a shame that the night cannot last forever

The Three of Swords

And so… it has come to this
Eyes narrowed, swords drawn as we stand
…back to back
I give we two my best, but it seems never
enough
Cannot get past our sordid past
Every little thing we both have done
Such a shame that we should walk this line
A thin border reflection of love versus hate
I can see it in your frigid eyes;
You despise me now
And I know that when you leave this all behind
That door will close for the final time
Leaving me once more to cry acid-bitter tears
Tears that you seem not to see; downpours of
discord
Oblivious as you turn away from me
And so… it has come down to this
Our bodies tense and rigid as we pretend to sleep
… lying back to back
My pillowslip dampened by that unseen river
As we drift restlessly into the solace of separate
dreams
While in the waking world it seems we have
nothing left to say

My words are choked off by helpless despair
We two both know that it is already over…
So why do we bother pursuing this lifeless
charade?
Our hearts both plea for the release,
Your own already secretly seeking out another
While my heart and soul are crying aloud
For the comfort and strength of only your
embrace
…are you so willing to let me go?
And so… it has now come to this
My heart pounds a fierce drum roll within my
throat
So sick, as I try to find the nerve
To give voice to the inevitable; to decide to end
all this
While you may not want the world outside
The eternal screens of our blessed fantasy realms
That world is beckoning to me
Your perpetual haze, of my own enabling
And what else is left now for me to do…
then to just simply leave you to keep pushing me
away?
All I want, all I have ever wanted
Was to eternally love, and be loved by only you
To believe without the constant assailing of
doubt
that you truly wanted, and loved me too
Your averted eyes; so oft-spoken pretty lies

Betray all of your hidden truths
(oh, and if I could only be as oblivious as you!)
While I am slowly dying inside
"Patience," croons a favorite refrain, "just wait it
out."
So that is exactly all I can do
Watching your eyes for all evident signs
As you try to repress the burning revulsion
within
Someday, my heart just might forgive you
For your cowardly escape without a spoken
good-bye
Though I suppose that makes little difference
… since I am already too far gone

Turmoil In Purgatory

In the aftermath of such devastating grief
This void of discord seems almost a relief
From your consistent pondering; ceaseless
circles within
Your silent mourning for all that might have
been

How blissful life was when I was blind to all of
this
Made sightless by our love and the sweet taste of
your kiss
So hard to recall now in this dismal state
A time where I did not feel so consumed by
self-hate

Pure love and light dim now, faded to a tease
Until all that is left are taunting memories
A thin and frayed bond of what used to seem
real
A faint whisper of the warmth that I used to feel

So cold now, as if Death's hand already clutches
my soul
A shucked husk; so empty… barren, desolate
hole

It hurts so just to look you in the eye
When every word upon your lips tastes to me a
lie

Aching, craving your touch, though it is all I
cannot bear
For even when we love, you are never truly
there
I can see it in your eyes, how your mind is so far
away
Even while in my embrace, your heart still runs
astray

Dreaming of any other, though you continue to
deny
Such sweet words upon your lips; then action
betrays the lie
I am so plagued by self-doubt, all I knew torn
asunder
Rooted here in helplessness, incessantly forced
to wonder:

Did you ever truly see me at all?
Will you care when my time comes to fall?
Fearing what is already lost, I simply cannot go
on
As I dare not to ask:
Will you even miss me when I'm gone?

April Fool (Mud Into Clay)

When soul feels like stone; heart like cold,
shapeless clay
Eyes are dry now, but are showing the strain
Of repressed tears that would fall like rain
Don't want to cry again today…
So anger seems an apt defense for pain

So oblivious while I am dying inside
I writhe with despair that I dare not mention
Desperately seeking some shred of attention
I reach for you, but am more often denied
Made forever unsure of your heart's intentions

I only wish that you had even a clue
That I could somehow just make you see
Exactly what it is you have done to me
By destroying my blissful, blind trust in you
You have, in turn, shattered the very core of me

Such careless gestures, did you even pause to
consider
Of just how I might feel when you push me
away?
While you reminisce fondly of your long gone
days

I sit idly by, feeling so useless and bitter
Mere tarnished bronze when compared to your
golden age

A repertoire of songs that I can no longer bear to
hear
Words and music that leads you to pine for
another
She, who denied you so many chances to love
her…
…and is THAT who you think of when you at
last draw me near?!
That name from your past that has always
caused me to shudder

Is that what you yearn for, while I fade from
your sight?
Crying in shadow as I sink into dreamless sleep
Among the wreckage of a love I fear only I still
keep
Will you ever even try to bring me back out into
the light…
Or simply keep you back turned to the tears that
I weep?

The Wreckage

Knew it was coming; saw it a thousand miles
away
A scent in the wind predicts the warning of utter
disarray
What have I done?
Oh, what have I done to me this time?
Forever doomed to this repetition…

To think I'd learned by now to leave ill enough
undone
Black chasms yawning wider, and the war is
never won
One side longing for completion
The other pleading for release
(we are who we are)

A shame you could never know how it all fits so
perfectly inside
To give my thought a Voice is madness, which I
cannot bear denied
A dream in dire need of waking; I thought you
could set me free
But the shackles still clench my soul
 Unyielding as they will always be

A steel albatross my only freedom; my one
window to the world
Someday they will find the wreckage of this
poor wretched little mad girl
We are only who we are… but just who are we?
What I do, what I see; who are you to judge me?
All that matters to only me; you can't understand
what you choose not to see
I am who I am, who I will always be
In this vast world of conformity, I just want to be
me

So what have I done?
Oh, what have I done to us this time?
I think I might have just wished the world
away…
…and it's too late to take back the rhyme.

Never Wander; Never Stray

Here I sit, stranded
Gritting mangled teeth against the thought
of going back to the horror show of work
awaiting me inside…
Here I sit, abandoned
In this temporary safe haven of my car,
too tempted to simply steal away into the night;
to drive away, just drive…
Here I sit, pondering
just for a minute, or two... or too many...
Chain-smoking on top of already pained lungs
while playing the radio game…
Here I sit, never wandering
wishing only to go home and be with you
to love you until I can no longer feel this pain…
Here I sit, in sad revelation
that you revel in my overnight shift hell
and you are in your truest moments of content
only when I am not there
Here I sit, in foolish contemplation
of our first night together; a hot night of near
impossible passion
eighteen long years ago to this very day… as if
you even care…
Here I sit, spurned and jaded

wondering if you know that I know you feel
that one long ago night might have been the
biggest mistake of your life…
Here I sit, devastated
torn apart by the previous thought
 for in my own life, you are my one true love
and my only light…
Here I sit, in speculation
mulling over the terrible notion of how your life
might improve
if I could only release you and set you free…
Here I sit, in isolation
knowing that I could never let you go
that I would be dead inside from the day you left
me…
Here I sit, deflated
feeling weak and useless; bleak and hopeless,
having failed all of the tests this life has thrown
my way…
Here I sit, in self-hatred
feeling that I have somehow failed you most of
all
and this hurts me more with every passing day…
Here I sit, in disdain
downing mental cocktails of discord and
contempt
consumed by revulsion and doubt
Here I sit, nearly insane

driven mad by the persistent belief that I never
truly had your love at all
so now I will have to re-learn to do without…
Here I sit, in absurd hope
dreaming of a future hopefully not too far away
a mutual retirement to our little house by the
sea…
Here I sit, and I cannot cope
tormented by the notion that my impending
fortune
is the only reason that you stay with me…
Here I sit, trying so hard
to dismiss this negativity; to convince myself
That only I am still haunted by your recent
mistakes…
Here I sit, in forlorn regard
reminding myself of the vows that we made;
richer or poorer, sickness and health
that marriage is always a matter of give and
take…
Here I sit, torn to shreds
sympathetic to the tortured Golem,
possessed by the dire need to find "the one
ring…"
Here I sit, so far out of my head
cursing my own carelessness; my scatterbrained
habits,
which are exactly what caused me to misplace
the Precious thing…

Here I sit, in expectant anxiety
while I wait for the sign I pleaded for;
the revelation of that memory now three years
passed…
Here I sit, hope lost in entirety
nearly mad with the desperate thought that this
curse of discord
will be only lifted when my Precious is found at
last…
Here I sit, in uncertain relief
our daily duties done, I sit beside you once more
where my heart belongs and my soul always
longs to be…
Here we sit, in covert belief
together but apart; in separate worlds on separate
screens
all the easier for you to not have to look at me…
Here we sit, in willful ignorance
until I slide alone into bed, all of my hurts
remaining unsaid
where I will lie awake until my anguish chases
me into my dreams…
And here we still sit, mutual indifference
upon a heap of empty, broken promises as we
pretend all is right in our little world…
…but nothing is ever what it seems…

Revelations of Dysphoria

Once, a connection so sweet
I believed in every promise, every whispered
endearment
Maintaining faith in my own naivety
Intentionally drawing myself blind
To all that I never wished to see

The passing of the years
Unity soured now, poisoned
Broken promises taste like tears
That fall unseen and unnoticed
A river in which I am doomed to drown
Hiding behind this smile facade

Contempt bred in familiarity
Long since, all hope extinguished
That you could ever even begin to see
All you've done, all you didn't do
Everything you once meant to me
...why couldn't you have just let me be?

Weary, so weary, I plod onward
So lonely, yet never alone
A failure in the eyes of infinity
Gazing into those eyes, I can only see
A reflection of all I an unable to be

As I weep for my own wasted heart

And as you might have guessed
Or you might have seen
These words are not from me to you
But are instead from you to me
Some, perhaps, from you to she
As the ever tedious maudlin kicks in
Your traitorous heart turns toward
All those shes that might have been
All the same to me… all I could never be

It makes no difference, your false apologies
Oozing lack of intent
Means not a thing to me
I begged for your interest, received only shame
Pleaded for understanding
In return, got only blame
Your inaction; my reaction
Take your hints and my lessons learned
And just fucking walk away
Leave me to my own dismay

All you do; all you say
And everything you don't
Piles upon these shattered remains
Growing heavier day by day
The unbearable weight will soon crush me
And then you will at last be free

Ode To Beloved

Center fracture; warped, twisted mirror
Contemplation flexes, both distant and nearer
With biased eyes, the reflection lies
Showing only a leper with a vicious mind
Consumed by faith in tragedy
Confused by thought with no strategy
She plummets, inevitable this falling
With no one to hear her desperate calling
Upon him, her entire world depends
With his departure, that world would end
Should she just stand idly by,
Watching him take his own life?
As he, selfishly, takes hers as well
Condemning them both to hell
When words are without voice,
Eternal slumber seems the saner choice
A whisper, a sigh… even a bloodcurdling
scream
To break the silence of this incessant black
dream
For him, she'd give the gift of her words
But for the conviction they would never be
heard
A siren's song falling upon deaf ears
Why won't he listen?- She needs him here!

His body still breathing, steady and slow
Showing no sign of the Death she feels in his
soul
So dark, so doomed without his inner light
She is losing her will to keep up this fight
His pulse is slow, once warm hands now so cold
Her touch will not thaw him, she has no control
Still, her arms cradle him in his frailty
As she cries out, "Killing you is killing me!
I love you still, how I love you so
My one, my only… please don't go!"
A weeping volcano, her bitter tears scald
All hope away as they incessantly fall
Consequence of his choice, their suffering is
eternal
Perpetual conviction to mutual inferno
For rather than leave him to face his Fate alone
She'll remain by his side on his desolate throne
 "My lover," she pleads, "my twin of soul.
Allow me to join you, and once more be made
whole."

Now captive within Death's savage embrace
Her beloved's eyes still see her… but veiled is
his face

Haunted

I saw your wasted form in the shadows
Watched as you crumbled to the ground
The soil you lie in consumes your body
A soul lost and never found
Your hands grope blindly for me
Though nothing remains inside
You do not see what you are reaching for
Since all we used to be has died
I want to feel your love once more
I long to put my fear behind
But I know your touch is mere illusion
Just a ghost within my mind
You there, hiding in the corner
The voice of your soul is pleading
A razor, cutting right through to my heart
And so I'm left here, scarred and bleeding
Again?!… No, not again!
I thought those dreams had met their end
I just wanted to show you true devotion
You don't need to know the reasons why
But your caress is just a mental image
Only a ghost within my mind
I lie here, unbidden images of you and I
Taste you; touch you; feel you…
We can escape that pain inside

Alas, you will never even see
All that you have done to me
I only wanted to try and save you
If I can't, then just let me be
The light sing-song of your chimes
All the riddles within your rhymes
Chains, not severed, that will forever bind
Me to the ghost within my mind
And I would pull you from those shadows
Unearth you from that soiled ground
But if it is only a waste of time
Then take your ghost out of my mind

The Island (Fathoms Deep)

Sun-kissed, all and everything
Light shimmers from every surface
Baking already bronzed skin
Beaming upon the oh-so happy crowds
Children shriek with maniacal joy
As they run for the tide line with their toys

All united with single-minded purpose
Enjoying a summer day by the sea
All save one: an island of her own
For even in such a peaceful scene as this
Her heart is leaden with persistent discord
Forever lonely; yet never alone
A dying Queen upon a rotting throne

The taste of salt upon her lips
Stinging in her eyes; tiny rivers upon her cheeks
Perhaps only the ocean air; or even just the sun's
harsh glare
Most likely her never ending flow of tears
Filled with despair, too much for her to bear
Her longing gaze strays out over the sea
The freedom of the eternal horizon
Oblivion, she muses, and can even spare a laugh
As she wonders how far she can swim

Would the surge take her out far enough
To escape this world built on despair?
Perhaps she'd befriend a dolphin
Or become dinner for a shark
… not like anyone would even care
She least of all; at last she'd be free
Swallowed by the horizon, or by the sea
Her pain only a distant memory

And the ocean- a picture perfect view
An example of the world's most dominant power
Fathoms deep is that great below
So relentless, the lure of the undertow
Creeping waves slap and play at the shoreline
Foaming, frothing, they slide forth and back
Creating their patterns for our eyes to behold
The sight touches the heart and pacifies the soul

Left behind footprints in the sand
Lead to the edge of the rolling tide
Caressed by the coolness of the sea's embrace
Kissed by the sun's rays upon her face
Not one single cloud floats in the canvass above
The sky, an artist's flawless blue
As perfect as the sepia sea of His eyes
So many fathoms deep, she dives

His voice an echo within the tumbling waves
Pleads for her to turn her course
She hears his warning, and hesitates
Thinks that even now, it may not be too late
From the deepest fathoms of her heart
She'd sent out a message, a cry for help
As mere symbols scraped into the sand
Yet enough to lend her a guiding hand

Discernment of Substance (Perception Is Everything)

Substance is friendship.
Substance is Love.
These two, when inseparable, are most
substantial
Those who deny themselves of either have
empty hearts with no substance
LIE is the(ir) substance; FAKE is the(ir)
substance.
Envy breeds spiteful hearts; spite breeds small
minds
Small minds have big mouths
That speak with no substance, and too often
break big hearts
Not even the Horned One Himself could sink to
such depths; He who is without substance
A journey through Sheol seems a vacation when
compared to such treachery...
And the Fallen Ones are EVERYWHERE,
spewing lack of substance

Substance is Strength.
Substance is Temperance.
Substantial is the incessant turning of the rumor
wheel.

While Karma is the Wheel that will eventually
break all.
I am fortunate with the blessings of both
friendship and love. That is substantial.
Too many are not so fortunate, and are sorely
lacking in substance.
These unfortunates are like the Fallen Ones
Whose own dull perception of substance is their
only everything
They know nothing of substance, or their own
lack thereof
They are worse than the Fallen, as they kneel
to lick the hooves of the Horned One
And He, made insane by his own lack of
substance
Would eat them alive for their blind ignorance
His eyes blazed a furious red from the top of the
Castle's highest Tower
…until he was cast down

Substance is the Castle; Substance is the Tower
Substantial is the land of Phantasia…
and the field of Roses that grow near the Falls
The Dreams of this land; the Chorus in the
Roses
The Emperor, and the High Council… they are
substantial
I am well met with the Council, and my beloved
Emperor

Fallen himself, now Ascended once more, after
millennia of my endless searching
 I once died in Sheol with his name upon my lips
and his child beneath my heart.
My hands painted red as the flames consumed
me
Fires set by His own declaration; my only crime
the attempt to redeem Him
I live again today in this world, insubstantial,
without Him by my side
But content with the knowledge that he is at last
free, and alive

Substance is Fantasy.
Substance is Illusion.
Substantial are these worlds lurking within my
imagination
I will go to these worlds someday...
But my work here in this world is not yet close
to the finish
The Council still needs the record to be set
straight
My beloved Emperor still needs his tale of
redemption told
And what of my own story of substance?
That of the lost Empress, the disgraced weaver
of dreams
The Muse who now fails to inspire even herself
As she descends into unbearable grief

No worry; no fear… she'll survive.
It's what she does; what she was made to do.

Substance is Survival.
Substance is Inspiration.
Substantial is NOT that stubborn pride that
refuses to allow me to cry for help
As I try to find my own way back out
Substance is light, just one tiny spark
To see those hard truths, and guide me back to
my destiny
Who I was, who I am now: a dreamer who paves
her path with words
I'll go crazy if I don't start writing again
I'll DIE if I don't start again!
Substantial is this revelation; knowing that spark
is NOT gone
But merely needs to be reignited

Substance is this gift of words that I shall not
squander
And force to become insubstantial
Substantial is the struggle of starting again
Relearning to love the agony of creation
Writing created the land of my dreams:
The Castle, the Tower, the High Council…
The Emperor, the Empress… they are
substantial.

The Magician is substantial. The Hanged Man is
substantial.
The High Priestess is substantial. The
Hierophant is substantial.
Even the Horned One is substantial, though
lacks substance Himself…
All have their stories to tell, their voices
Sing in the chorus of the field of Roses
Beckoning me to take up my sword once more

The voice of my Mother, most substantial
So loud in that Chorus, as she summons me back
to life
Reminding me of who I am; who I ought to be
The Lovers or The Three of Swords?
The Empress or The Fool?
Foolish to some it may seem… but these
questions are substantial.
And require answers of substance
Substance is knowing my Mother is still with
me.
Substance is knowing that she is still proud.
The Castle, while in grave disrepair from my
neglect
Still stands, and that is substantial.
The Horn of Redemption has been sounded
And old worlds are mended and reborn…
Substance!
At long last, I have found it again.

At long last, I have come home…
To recover all that has been lost

The chorus of the Roses sing on, and will do for
eternity
Providing substance to all who would listen
And the Eyes peering out from the Tower are red
no more
For the Horned One no longer haunts my heart
Instead, twin lamps of singed copper gaze down
upon me
Alight with a substantial smirk of challenge
As my Emperor's voice rejoins the chorus
Savage, yet gentle… taunting, yet cajoling
He calls out to His Empress Muse; his
de-throned Queen:
"When I was Fallen, it was you who lifted me
from me knees,
Now rise yourself, and find your substance in
me.
It's a long, weary climb up here to the top
And, once you begin, you must never stop."

Substance is mounting that winding stair
Substance is determination conquering the fear
One step at a time…
Indeed, a seemingly endless climb
To redemption I'm not even sure I'll find
Substance…

With His voice in my ear, I am fearless
Substance...
Within His embrace I will be whole once more
Home again at last.
...Substance.

Belated

Lying restless in bed, she's alone again
Not much surprise here, it's always the same
Tattered pictures of her Beloved's face
Hang in her mind, painstakingly framed
Silent tears of anguish and fright
Prevent her from falling asleep at night
While she still longs to believe that these dreams
are her destiny
And this feeling of doubt is just his way of
testing
His eyes in her soul; she is haunted
Radio games; she is taunted
Faithful and lonely, she waits for a sign
Seeking solace she knows that she'll never find
Waves in the sea churn the light of the moon
The wind whispers through the grass-covered
dunes
Just whose will was it that guided her hand
As she scraped a symbolic phrase in the sand?
This plea, she knows, somehow He received
Though it falls against all she'd been taught to
believe
One wish confided to candle flames
More long hours of playing the radio game
So many loves have come, and then gone

Even now, love for one of them still lingers on
But it doesn't even begin to compare
To the hunger she reads in his coffee-toned glare
She has fallen so hard for the strength that He
gives
An impossible love, because of who He is
This faith has become so tired and strained
But still, as she plummets, she is calling His
name

Belated… that one word, so refined
The refrain a harsh echo through her mind
It seems the story of both of their lives
All the times they have lived and then died
They have been down this road before
And will tread this thorny path once more
Growing accustomed to the lesions
That brand their skin with each passing season
His words sting as an accusation
As she faces Him in forced confrontation
"Do you even have the good grace to cringe
After you've denied me for so long in your
self-pity binge?"
Her response, a slow smile of bemusement
As she considers his cadence of amusement
For she knows he taunts her not with cruelty
But because it is simply his honor and duty
For it is not the first time she has lost faith in
herself

Nor the last she will call upon him for help
He smiles at her, the relief clear in His eyes
Once lost in self-doubt; she has finally realized
The renewed light in her eyes; dawn of
revelation
Her faith in His guidance is His source of
salvation
This connection she'd tried so hard to achieve
Failed only when she refused to believe
Yet, as trepidation once more intervenes
Her conscience is heavy, as she understands
what this means
There are no words for the harm she has caused
Him
First haunting his heart, then vanishing on a
whim
Her tears burst forth and she drops to her knees
Begs His forgiveness in stammered apologies
His touch reassuring as he dries her tears
And pulls her back to her feet, drawing her near

"Your denial did set us back a bit, true
But make no mistake, love… it was ME who
called YOU.
I summoned you when I needed to heal
Then you answered my call, let me in, made me
real
Not your burden alone, this late realization

So as we part ways once more, let's do with
some consolation
To the end of Time itself, you and I are Fated
Perhaps not this time, though… our revelation
belated
But I beg you to remember, even when we're
apart
You are always with me; never far from my
heart."
Now wakened from this impossible vision
She carries on unburdened by indecision
For she knows now, in this life, or in another
She'll find Him waiting, her One, her Lover

Those Voices of Recluse

Colors to stain the white washed canvass
 Words a channel; at last flowing free
Conquering the terror of an empty page
As this life so often seems to be
I stumble upon a few rare kindred souls
Points of light in the dim sea of humanity
Ones who share that unfathomable faith
That not all souls are destined to conformity

Within the midst of this simmering society
They stand typically apart and alone
Secluded from those who cling solely to reason
Reaching for vague objectives; not all intentions
known
I can accept that the world does not want us
Cast aside as insane or heretic; branded as
lunatic freak
Growing strong, the keen instinct of survival,
and we rise still
While the rest slaughter one another other in the
streets

Developmental focus upon the future, the
constant
Expedition of bigger, better, faster, more

The blind ignorance of the present will be our
undoing
As society shuts out its heart's human core
So I clutch tight my soul's free spirited roots
And with the kindred ones join hands
In unity, though scattered, our voices call out as
one
Echoes reverberating across all lands

Through it all, I am always seeking, pleading
For my Emperor, whose own siren beckons me
His enchanted hands lock as they fold around
The last untainted piece of my heart
So secure, and only He holds the key

Rejuvenation

Faint light creeps through these windows
In shades of gray as dawn lays its touch upon the
earth
Cold now, as the wind plays its lonely, mournful
song
I shiver and pull the blankets up tight to my chin
Though nothing can soothe the chills away
As well as would your warm embrace
Those arms that I long to have around me now
I think of you, fathoms of realms away
My Mind's Eye sees you upon your Emperor's
Throne
And I wonder if you could also be wishing that I
was there
So strange, how lifetimes of absence
Truly makes our hearts grow more fond
I smile to myself in the low light of early
morning
Reflecting upon your strength as you lift me
A wonderful feeling of elation, so great
That with words, it can not even be defined
Never before has such emotion touched my soul
Almost frightening with its intense clarity
And I know there will never be another for me…

That it was always you; the love I have seen in
my dreams
A light in the darkness; a touch of warmth to an
icy heart
The very lifeline in my realms of insanity
I could write all of this… spanning over a
thousand pages
And still not come even close
To describing the depths of your significance to
me
And the Mind's Eye can see you smiling now…
A rueful grin of amusement; that smirk I so
adore
Your head shaking as you reply, "But I am only
just me!"
As if, love, you did not really believe,
That's all I would ever need you to be!
It's no small accomplishment, when my lips
curve into a smile
But a miracle you create, by simply being who
you are
For the sun to break free from the dark cloud of
my thoughts
Though it may be only one moment out of time,
That thin ray of pure light is enough to keep me
strong
In a world so otherwise cold and gray
The overcasts burst open, rain falls in merciless
torrents

Dampening the spirits of one even as bright,
As incessantly strong as you are to me
And I wonder… could I courteously extend the
same helping hand
As you do when Life's general madness
swooped down to claim me?
Would my kiss, my embrace, soothe away your
frustrations
As your tower of infallible strength shelters me?
With these silly poems I structure, or even
stories of novel length
… I could never write enough…
or broadening horizons to expand and culture
myself
… I could never learn enough…
even hunting online for trivial, materialistic
objects
… I could never spend enough…
to come anywhere close to an equal justification
of the depth of my love and appreciation for you
and, my love, that is exactly why I do
all of these things I so love doing for you!
For just one of those trademark, impish grins
I would gladly turn over both heart and soul
To hear your laughter, or to feel the touch of
those magic hands
Is both a joy and a privilege to one so sullen as I
If there are times when I lose sight of such
elation

It is only because I've not known this feeling
before
So sometimes it seems there's nothing else for
me to do
But to question my self-worth… do I truly
deserve you?
What wonderful deed is it that I've done
To have you by my side through the struggle of
each passing day?
Could it possibly be that my hand, extended in
love
Is what helps to keep your own darkness at bay?
Whatever the reason this luck had befallen me
I am eternally grateful
To have you as the very life of my heart
So please, let me know… where should I begin
To return to you the same light that you have
shown me?
At those points when your mood seems
particularly low
All I can offer is some friendly advice:
You should never take a willing, headlong
plunge
Into the black abyss of insanity
For it is a long, long tumble with no cushioned
landing
And an even longer climb back up to the top
But should you jump, regardless of this advice

I can't promise to catch you, but I will promise
to try
And if the worse case scenario should play itself
out
Then I would soon follow your plummet down
For I'd much rather jump with you; your hand in
mine
Than to carry on alone in this dismal world

So I take this notebook to bed, expressing the
unthinkable
The Fear of losing you to great for either words
or tears
There is no other for me; nor would there ever
be
All that I am now would go with you
My love; my light…
All that is sweet to this bitter soul
Never doubt who you are to me
Everything that is beautiful to these tired eyes
Sees its first light through you
All the warmth, all the comfort
The sheer bliss of true contentment
Is when I am there by your side, snug in your
embrace
And my heart will live there forever more…
So I guess, then, the true purpose of these
rambling words
Is to thank you for just being you

A Shadowed Soul Enlightened

Intimidated by this blank page, this empty sea
Of blue-lined whiteness, staring up at me,
patronizing
Silently daring me to achieve the near
impossible goal:
That of finding words deep and meaningful
enough
To vocalize the love I feel for you
So difficult, you see, to describe emotion as
great as this
One that I've never known before, nor believed
could ever exist
Within a soul so soured; so bitterly cynical as
mine own
It seems such a strange and foreign concept to
me
How even the most simplest of gestures
Such as that much adored smirk, or a casual
brushing of fingertips
Could instill within me such an intense reaction
Heart pounding a thunderous beat; stomach
fluttering with twinges of desire
And this soul, once so frigid, has thawed with
the warmth of your touch

And suddenly, I've become the woman I've
always wanted to be
Someone who, in spite of her outward
ill-tempered appearance
Is finally allowing herself to feel worthy of this
true elation
No easy task, that of basking in the light of
contentment
For after so many years of hurt and discontent
I'd learned to accept loneliness as it's own cruel
Fate
Destined to love, but only alone…
Nights forever spent drowning in meaningless
hope
Wrapped in the solace and dismal comfort of a
dream
That I have finally managed to somehow take
with me
As I emerged into the reality of the waking
world

By the wonderful virtue of your clear, blatant
honesty
And the calm strength of your infallible patience
I've been set free from my chains of inevitable
doom
So this heart, once so heavy with trepidation and
despair

Is now weightless and buoyant with the love
you've shown me
For years, I could only dream of this chance
Never quite believing it might actually come to
pass
Now, that it has happened, by either Fate or just
blind luck
I find myself so amazed by the simple truth of it
all
For once, I'm exactly where I need to be, and
have all that I could want
…All I have ever wanted…
Since that very first glimpse into those
chrome-kissed eyes
And by coaxing out the better side within me
You have helped to heal and cleanse this weary
soul

And my hope now is in your intentions to stay…
For the only time I feel truly whole and alive
Are those moments when I am so blissfully
wrapped
Within the snug cocoon of your embrace
And having you, as my true love, is of such
great assurance to me
That it would take the strength of well over ten
thousand men
To make me ever let you go

True Calling

Will you come away with me tonight?
O'er the hunting grounds, aloft in flight
Against the odds; against the tide
We'll interlace as the stars align
Phantasm and reality
A line too obscure to see
Pull back the veil; peer in between
And that's where you'll find me

I realize it was you
All along, I think that I knew
Where it counts, deep down inside
I felt the truth behind the lie
Let's cross illusion's narrow line
And lay our masks aside
We play this game of riddle and rhyme
But those eyes you could never hide

They always said we'd be a perfect mess
The Lycanthrope versus the Lioness
So detached; our separate paths
Only to come 'round again and reconnect
All the tears for the time we've wasted
All the long years of glamour games
Tried to deny it, but underestimated
How the zephyr will always feed the flames

And I realize it was you
All along, I think that I knew
Where it counts; deep down inside
I felt the truth behind the lie
Crossing illusion's narrow line
Laying all our masks aside
Playing these games of riddle and rhyme
But those eyes you could never hide

So come away with me tonight
We'll leave the disparagement behind
True love and unity; mutual lunacy
Our perfect mess defined
We'll thumb our noses at the odds defied
Compensating for all the misspent time
It doesn't matter what we once were inside
For I am yours, and you are mine

And I knew it was you!
Now I know that I always knew
Where it counts, deep down inside
I felt the truth behind the lie
We've crossed illusion's narrow line
And have laid all our masks aside
No more games of riddle and rhyme
'Cuz those eyes you can never hide

Moon-drenched nights while on the prowl
Consumed by the blood's primordial call
Within the infinite chorus, your lonely howl
That one unique voice I will hear above all
No matter how high I ascend, how far away I
may roam
You alone have the power to hail me home
When you're lost, or simply feeling alone
Just open up and howl me home

Duplicity

Could it possibly that somewhere…
Within the chaotic midst of Life's general
deception
That the soul in there…
YOU could be my every Rule's one exception
To me, it is a mystery…
Of why I choose the heap these torments upon
myself
A circle of history…
Incessantly repeats as though I were living as
someone else
Far too many miles…
Of ceaseless roads I've traveled alone
I see the fading smiles…
On your lips, reflecting my own
I wonder if you, too, can see…
The simplicity of this infatuation
But I know that it could never be…
The realization comes coupled with desolation
I wonder if you are hearing…
Any of the messages I am sending to you
And if you know that I am fearing…
That tainting your soul is all I would do
My heart's true intentions…
Never seem to be expressed by my actions

And I will never be able to mention…
How within me you stir up a strange reaction
A whirlwind of emotion…
So unfamiliar the scent and taste
This soul withers in corrosion…
From acting too often out of haste
My beaten and tattered wings…
Draw me to an angel's embrace, unbroken
And my consciousness sings…
With the words forever unspoken
In the new awareness…
Of what these transcribed phrases really mean
I sense the unfairness…
To you, and I must now come clean
I am lost in duplicity…
Truly in love not with one, but with two
And I long for the simplicity…
To break through this confusion by falling to you

Sanctuary

Rapturous dreams of my Obsession
Mingle and linger in perfection
Sugar and rose, the scents so sweet
Within the folds of rumpled sheets
Still warm from our heated skin
Famished still, I breathe her in
Bodies fusing, limbs entwining
Soft ropes around me, gently binding
I tremble with the ache of need
Consumed by my own unholy greed
To be the knight that sets her free
To have her here now in this bed with me
Whispered plans of midnight meetings
More precious than vows, however fleeting
Prospective lazy Sunday afternoons
More dear than a lifetime, yet pass too soon
Together, such scant few minutes spent
Worth hours forfeit to lonely torment
One moment's embrace in her sheltering wings
Merits thousand day anguish that her absence
brings
Oblivious to how wretched and alone
I was, until she came into my home
Illumination of these dim castle walls
Echoes of her laughter haunting my halls

Smoldered sapphires; a wry twist of smile
Hide secrets of her suffering, an endless trial
Of a devotion unnoticed, a kindness neglected
The pure gift of her words, too often rejected
She bears constant misuse from a foolish man
Who, blind to the miracle he holds in his hands,
Incessantly berates her, and tears her apart
And smothers the flame of her golden heart
That very same fire I so long to capture
Will she ever surrender to her soul's call for
rapture?
My Goddess, repressed by the weight of her fear
She is her true self only when she is here
My one wish is to somehow make her see
To teach her even as she teaches me
Value of worth; more precious than gold
Chaos arousing this dejected soul
A typhoon of joy to which I gladly resign
Our moments so sacred they need not be defined
Just live here in this now, disregard what comes
next
For what I am already feeling, her eyes do
reflect
Logic cries out that it's too much, too soon
But the more I deny, the more I am consumed
So I implore her, my Goddess, to allow me to be
All that she is to me; sweet sanctuary